桂林山水

王桯生摄影集

GUILIN SCENERY
PHOTO COLLECTION BY
WANG WU SHENG

广西师范大学出版社

责任编辑: 唐长兴
装帧设计: 邬永柳　唐长兴
封面题字: 吴作人
英文翻译: 周　济
日文翻译: 罗清云

桂　林　山　水
——王梧生摄影集

广西师范大学出版社出版　　　　　　　　　邮政编码:541001

(广西桂林市中华路36号)

中国外文局桂林对外文化图书交流中心发行

深圳雅昌彩色印刷有限公司印刷

*

开本:850×1168　1/16　　　　印张:6

1997年6月第一版　　　　　　　　1997年6月第一次印刷

印数:0001－5000册

ISBN7－5633－2414－3/J·082

(平)005800　　　　(精)006800

一瞬之间
至物无穷

梧生同志雅正

乙丑 光敏

老收天下事境

一九八八年夏应
王樾生属书为 [印章]
怀人 [印章]

序

　　苍莽神州，有水皆秀，无山不雄，尤以桂林景色甲天下，容阳刚阴柔一体，合宇宙英灵一炉。春天如梦幻中幼女，身掩霞纱，漫舞榕荫，婀娜烂漫；夏日似瑞凝少妇，洋溢生命狂喜，葱茏茂郁，滴翠沁芳；金秋若才高八斗诗仙，随手点化，无不微妙；温冬像沉思古哲，儒家热肠，道家高洁，魂景相抱，回味无穷。加上幽洞、奇石、花雨、彩雾、清风、浮岚、飞瀑、灵泉、古碑、朝月、夕阳，瞬息百变，仪态万方。月挂冰盘，星星漂于江底，竹摇凤尾，帆帆载满渔歌。游客一见钟情，终生不忘。古往今来，多少墨客无言，画师搁笔！

　　吾友王君梧生何幸生于仙乡，饱餐漓江神乳，看醉阳朔云飞。扪读桂海碑林，心师前修；吟断韩愈佳句，意逐征鸿。数十年间勤研摄影，酷爱美学。眷恋故地，苦乐两忘，以赤子澄怀，艺人悟性，奔波山道，往返群峰。广搜文献传说，品味风土个性。常访老农船夫，敬之如父兄。风霜心路，见闻体验，存于镜底，刹那便成永恒。沙里淘金，八千精选九七，迎香港回归，献有缘识者。小序喝道，遥唤护法知音，艺海无涯，予更有待梧生。

柯文辉

1997年4月26日

序　文

　　そうぼうたる神州では、水のあるところはみな綺麗で、雄大でない山がない。もっとも優れているのが桂林の景色は天下随一である。頑丈なものと柔らかいものが溶け合って、宇宙の英霊を合わせている。春は夢幻の中の少女のように、身に肩掛けをして、気の行くままに踊って、しなやかで美しくて爛漫である。夏は凝視している若い婦人のように生命の狂喜に溢れていて、青青と生い茂って香しいです。秋は才気に溢れる詩仙のように、思うままに点景を添えていて、微妙でないものがなし。冬は沈思している先哲のように儒家の熱情と道家の高潔で魂と景色を抱き合って、反芻してはかりしれないです。その上、奥ゆかしい洞窟、まれに見る奇石、四季折折花盛り、色とりどりの霧、清い風、浮いている嵐気、飛瀑、清い泉、古い碑文、朝の月、夕日、またたく間に変化していて、姿態が非常に美しいです。月は透き通っている皿のように空に掛けて、星は川底に漂い、鳳尾竹は揺らめき、セーリングシップから漁歌が聞こえ、遊客は一見ぼれして生涯忘れられない。昔から今まで、多少の文人墨客が黙っていて、多少の画家も筆を擱いたでしょう。

　　私の友人の王梧生氏は、仙境に生まれていて何と幸せでしょう、夕食は漓江の神乳を飲み、ちらちら陽朔の雲の摂影に没頭しています。桂海碑林の碑文を撫でて読み、心の中の師としての修業が事前に終了しました。韓愈の佳句を繰り返し吟味して、遠征に出掛けている大雁を追いつこうと考え、数十年に亘って摂影の技術研究に励み、美学を深く愛し、故郷を懐かしんでいて、苦楽をともに忘れてしまい、赤子の清らかな澄みきっている懐と芸術家の見込みで、小道と群峰の間を行ったり来たりして苦心奔走しています。広範に文献を集め、風土と個性を味わい、つねに年寄りの農民と船人を尋ね、父兄のように尊敬し、辛酸を嘗め尽くし、心の道での見聞と体験をレンズの中に収め、またたく間に永久不変になりました。砂金を選り分けるように、八千枚ほどの作品の中から97枚を精選して、香港の祖国復帰を迎え、ご縁のある見識の高い人士に献上します。この小さい序文で先払いをすることは遥かかなたの護法の知音を呼びかけます。芸術は海と空のように果てしなくて、私は更に梧生を期待しています。

柯文辉

1997年4月26日

1. 象山雄姿 1.Imposing Sight of Elephant Hill　1.象山の雄姿

PREFACE

Viewing all over the Divine Land, where there is river must be beautiful and where there is mountain must be magnificent, but among them all, the Guilin landscape scenery is acclaimed as the crown of all landscapes under the Heaven, which integrates the Magnificence of Yang and the softness of Ying as one entity, compounding the universal beautiful spirits in such a panorama. In the Spring the scenery here looks like a fancy girl, who wears a sun–glow dressing, slowly dancing under Banyan trees, so romatic and charming; whereas in the summer days it looks like an amorous lady, full of hilarity in life, emitting youthfulness and fragrancy; in the golden autumn the scenery seems to be a talent poet who can make rhyme at ease, each poem sentence is always excellent; in the warm winter it looks like an ancient sage, with Confucian enthusiastic hospitality, and with Daoist school's solitude and exclusiveness. The spirit integrated with the scenery, which make you thinking and reviewing boundlessly. In addition, there are deep caves, grotesque rocks, drizzling, sun–glow mist, fresh breeze, floating clouds and mist in the hills, water fall, spring, ancient steles, cold moon in the morning and sunset, all these are changeable at any moment, forming hundred and thousand of fabulous scenes. The moon hang on as freeze pan, whereas stars floating under the bottom of the river, the bamboo' waves its head as if a phoenix swings its tail, and fishing boats sound triumphantly folk song. The scenes are so impressive that tourists shall never forget it in their all life whenever they see them. The scenery is in such wonderful change that since ancient time it makes don't know how many celebrities could not say more about it and how many painters feel hesitating in drawing it up.

As a friend of mine, Mr. Wang Wusheng is lucky to be born in such a fairyland, bred and grown up by the spirit of the Lijiang river, quite familiar with the clouds floating over the Yangshuo. He read through the Guihai Stele Forest, imitating the ancient sages' style and learned by heart the famous poems by Han Yu, who was a famous poet in Tang Dynasty, cherishing the hope and intention to conquer broad masses in artistic circle. For this purpose he spent several tens of years for researching photography, supported by his ardent love to aesthetics. He loves his hometown so much that he often forgets the working hardness and takes no care of entertainment, to climb up and down or go and come in zigzag road among the hills and peaks, just for the sake of art, and conducting by his artist emotion only. He has gathered legends from vast documentary records, tasting and meditating the folklore personalities. He often pays visit to the old peasant and fishing man, regarding them as his brother or father. Through such a weather–beaten experience and heart to heart communication, he preserves what are most impressive which he has seen and informed, into his camera, by snapping–shot and thus making it to be perpetual forever. Now he has chosen 97 pieces of outstanding works from more than eight thousands of his photographs, for celebrating the date of the return of Hong Kong to the Motherland, as a present to the photograph–loving people. I wrote this preface for beating gongs to clear the way only, expecting that friends keenly appreciative of Wang's talent to have this photo selection. the artistic sea is boundless, people are expecting for more from Mr. Wang Wusheng.

Ke Wenhui
April 26th, 1997

2. 伏波山容貌
2.Scenery of Fubo Hill
2.伏波山の容姿

3.叠彩山之夏
3.Summer Day of Diechai Hill
3.畳彩山の夏

6.龙头山烟霞
6.Rosy Mist in Dragon Head Hill
6.龍頭山の煙霞

7.峰丛神光

7.Holy Light among Clustered Peaks

7.峰叢の神光

8. 群峰旭日
8.Sun Rising over Peak Forest
8. 群峰の旭

9.春暖花桥
9.Warm Spring of Flower Bridge
9.春の麗らかの花橋

10.雾漫奇峰
10.Mist Spreading over Grotesque Peaks
10.霧が立ちこめる奇峰

11.田家河晨曦
11.Morning Sun Ray in Tianjiahe
11.田家河の朝の日光

12.漓江情韵
12.Folklore Rhyme of the Lijiang River
12.灘江のおもむき

13.翠竹山影
13.Inverted Reflection of Bamboo Hill
13.翠竹と山の影

14.山城阳朔

14.Hilly Town--Yangshuo

14.山城陽朔

15.青峰倒影

15.Inverted Reflection of Green Hills

15.青峰の倒影

16.漓江红帆
16.Red Canvas on the Li River
16.灕江の赤い帆

17. 浪石览胜
17.Wave Rock Scenery
17. 浪石絶景

18.晓雾
18.Morning Mist
18.朝霧

19.黄布晨韵
19.Morning Rhyme in Huangbu
19.黄布の朝の韻

20.兴坪山水

20.Landscape of Xingping

20.興坪の山水

21.疑是仙境在凡间

21.Wondering in a Fairyland on the Earth

21.下界の仙人の境と疑う

22.骆驼过江
22.Camel Crossing the River
22.駱駝の川渡り

23.云烟争艳

23.Clouds and Mist competing for Charming

23.雲煙艶を争う

24.下龙秀色
24.Beautiful Scenery of Xialong
24.下龍の美しい景色

27. 漓江渔火

27.Fishing Light on the Li River

27. 灕江漁火

28.如梦漓江水
28.Dreaming Flow of the Li River
28.夢のような灕江の水

29.漁村早渡
29.Morning in the Ferry of a Fishing Village
29.漁村の早渡り

30.冠岩仙境
30.Fairyland in Crown Rock
30.冠岩仙境

31. 奇峰春姿

31. Spring Pose of a Grotesque Peak

31. 奇峰の春姿

32.家在画图中

32.Home in a Painting

32.家は絵の中に

33.兴坪朝板山
33.Chaoban hill in Xingping
33.興坪の笏山

34.江畔小景
34.A Glimpse by the River Bank
34.江畔の小景

35.阳朔烟雨

35.Drizzle and mist in Yangshuo

35.陽朔煙雨

36.夏漓江
36.Summer Day on the Li River
36.夏の灕江

37.雪狮岭朝霞
37.Snow Lion Hill Facing Morning Sun Glow
37.雪獅嶺のあさやけ

38.漓江夜色
38.Night Scene of the Li River
38.灘江の夜色

39.峰丛脚下住人家
39.Homes at the Foot of Peak Forest
39.峰叢の麓に人家

40.争辉
40.Striving for Highlight
40.輝きを競う

41.夕照兴坪

41.Sunset in Xingping

41.興坪の夕日

42.云漫山浮
42.Clouds Flowing and Hills Floating
42.雲が立ちこめ山が浮かぶ

43.波光渔影
43.Wave flash and Fishing Image
43.波の光漁の影

44.漓江浪石
44.Waving Rock in the Li River
44.灘江の浪石

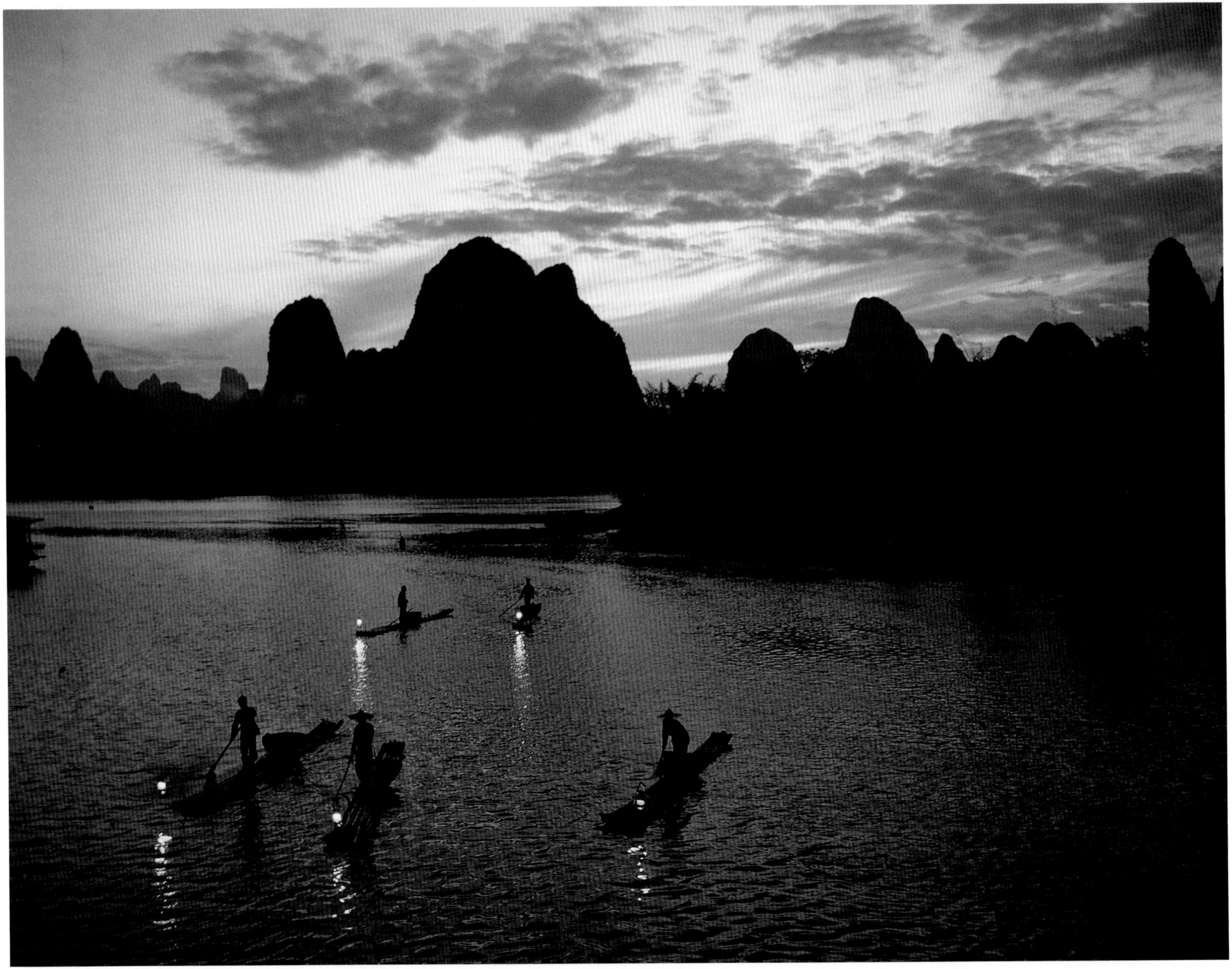

45 秋水渔歌

45 秋の漁歌

45 Fishing Folk Song at Water in Autumn

47. 榕江春云
47. Spring Clouds in the Rong River
47. 溶江春の雲

48.山村暮色
48.Mountainous Village in Dusk
48.山村の夕やみ

49.漓江捞丝草
49.Gathering Fishing
Grass in the Li River
49.灕江の水草を取る

50.马蹄峰云霞
50.Glowing Clouds and
Mist in Mati Peak
50.馬蹄山の霞

51.罗带玉簪
51.Ribbon and Emerald Hairpin
51.薄絹の帯とかんざし

52.僧尼山下
52.At the Foot of Monk & Nun Hill
52.僧尼山の下

55.春花怒放
55.Flowers Blossoming in the Spring
55.春花咲き競う

56.大地回春
56.Land Waking up for Spring
56.大地に春が蘇る

59.漓江座笔峰
59.Pen-rack Hill by the Li River
59.灕江の筆先の峰

60.春晓
60.Early Spring
60.春暁

61. 小憩

61. A Group of Hills competing for beauty

61. いっぷく

62.八仙过海
62.The Eight Immortals Crossing the Sea
62.八仙人の海渡り

63.汲
63.Drawing Water
63.汲む

64.高田月亮山
64.Moon Hill in Gaotian
64.高田の月亮山

65.漓水童真
65.Naive Children by the Lijiang River
65.灕江の童貞

66.梦幻花桥
66.Fancy Flower Bridge
66.夢幻の花橋

67.刘三姐古榕传情
67.Third Sister Liu expressing Love under the Old Banyan Tree
67.劉三姐の古榕樹での流し目

68.古榕伴清流
68.A Clear Stream surrounding Old Banyan Tree
68.古榕樹に清流

69.福利小景
69.A Glimpse of Fuli
69.福利の小景

70.漓江晨曦
70.Morning Sun Ray on the Li River
70.灘江の朝の日光

71.漓水晨风
71.Morning Breeze on the Li River
71.灕水の朝風

72.凤尾迎宾
72.Phoenix's tail welcoming Guest
72.迎賓の鳳凰竹

73.漓江胜览

73.Sightseeing on the Li River

73.灕江の素晴らしい景観

74. 烟雨漓江
74.Mist and Raining on the Li River
74. 煙雨の灘江

75. 三山冬姿

75. Winter scenery of Three Hills

75. 三つの山の冬姿

76.驼峰初夏

76.Summer Day of Camel Hill

76.駱駝峰の初夏

77.高田春绿
77.Spring Scenery in Gaotian
77.高田の春緑

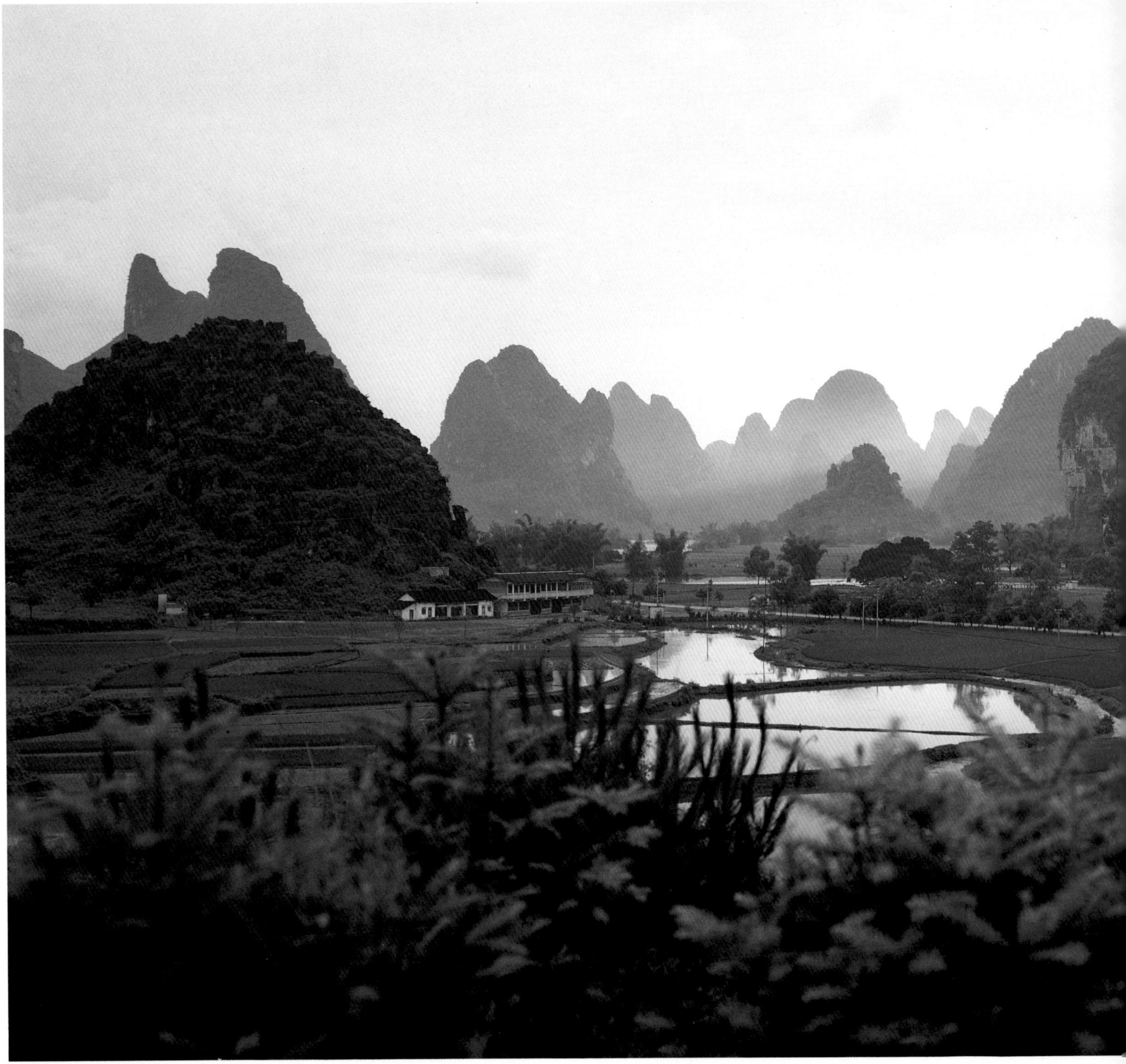

78.漓江神曲
78.Godlike Rhythm of the Li River
78.灕江の神曲

79.漁島
79.Fishing Island
79.漁島

80.青峰倒影山浮水
80.Inverted Reflection of Peak Forest and Hills Floating on the Water
80.青峰倒影して山水に浮かぶ

81. 远眺七星山

81. Viewing Seven-star Hill from Long Distance

81. 七星山の遠望

82. 流彩飞霞

82.Drifting Rosy Clouds and Mists

82. 彩雲が流れ霞が飛ぶ

83.灵渠滚水坝
83.Spilling Dam of Qin Canal
83.霊渠運河のダム

84.漓水行舟
84.Cruising Boat on the Li River
84.灘水を行く船

90.漓江抱兴坪

90.Xingping Enclosed by the Li River

90.灘水に抱かれる興坪

91.蘑菇亭冬雪
91.Winter Snow covering
Mushroom Pavilions
91.あずまやの冬雪

92.尧山朝阳
92.Morning Sun in Yau Mountain
92.尧山の朝目

93.漓江垂钓
93.Fishing at the Lijiang River
93.灘江の魚釣

94.桂花飘香
94.Heavy Osmanthus Aroma in the Air
94.馨しい金モクセイ

95.奇峰红叶

95.Grotesque Peak and Red Leaves

95.奇峰の紅葉

作者简介

王梧生，1942年生，是国内外著名摄影艺术家。其摄影作品精湛，尤以风光见长。作品格调清雅，构图别致，用光考究，意境深远。在国内外发表作品近万幅，百多次在国内外摄影艺术沙龙和展览中入选展出并获金、银、铜牌奖。发表《试论桂林山水摄影造型技巧》等20多篇论文，出版专著《现代风光摄影技巧》及《桂林山水——王梧生摄影集》等五本，以及桂林、漓江、阳朔系列明信片70多套。

王梧生现为中国摄影家协会会员、中国艺术摄影学会广西分会副会长、桂林艺术摄影学会会长、桂林市展览馆馆长，连续两届被评为桂林市专业技术拔尖人材。国家高级摄影师。

作者のあらまし

王梧生，1942年生まれ、国内外で著名な摂影芸術家である。その摂影した作品は精致で美しい、特に景色の摂影に長じています。作品のスタイルがすっきりしていて、構図が新鮮で一風変わっています。そして、光線の使い方に重んじていて、情調が深遠です。これまで、国内外で作品を一万枚近く発表しました。そのうち百回あまり国内外の摂影芸術サロンと展示会に入選されまして、金、銀、銅のメダルを勝ち取りました。それから、「桂林山水の摂影造形についての技法を論ずる」等20篇の論文を発表しました。そして、「現代の景色摂影の技法について」の専門著書と「桂林山水——王梧生摂影集」等の本五冊及び桂林、漓江、陽朔等の絵葉書シリーズ70余セットを出版しました。

現在は中国摂影家協会会員、中国芸術摂影学会広西分会副会長、桂林芸術摂影学会会長、桂林市展示館館長、2年も続けて桂林市の専門技術抜粋人材に選ばれ、国の高級摂影師である。

BRIEF INTRODUCTION TO THE AUTHOR

Wang Wusheng, born in 1942, is a famous artistic photographer in China and being well known abroad also. His photographic works are exquisite, particularly those works characterized by landscape and scenery. The style of his work is fine and elegant, the make up of picture is unique, the light flash is applied carefully, and the significance of picture is always profound.

He has published his phographic works at home and abroad for ten thousands pieces proximately, more than one hundred times being elected to display in artistic photograph Saloons and exhibitions at home and abroad, and obtained the prizes of the Gold, Silver and Bronze respectively. Published the thesis " On Photographic Make – up Technique of Guilin Langscape " and other feature articles for 20 – plus. Published the specific works for five books, such as " Contemporary Photographic Technique for Landscape and Scenery ", and " Guilin Landscape——Selected Photographic Works by Wang Wusheng ", and published series of postcards reflecting the scenery in Guilin, the Lijiang River and Yangshuo for more than 70 sets.

Mr. Wang Wusheng is a member of the Photographer Association of China, vice chairman of the Guangxi Branch of the Artistic Photography Society of China, chairman of the Guilin Artistic Photography Society, the Director of Guilin Exhibition Gallery. He was elected for twice successively as one of outstanding professional personnel in Guilin. He is entitled the Senior Photographer of the state.

后　记

　　当这本摄影集面世的时候,已是香港回归祖国、结束百年沧桑屈辱之日。以这本集子迎接这一喜庆佳节,正是作者和编辑人员编辑出版这个集子的初衷。

　　97这个吉祥的数字,无疑是中华民族历史的光辉页码,全世界的炎黄子孙都将为之骄傲,并世代铭记。作者从上万幅影作中精选出97幅佳作奉献给广大摄影爱好者和国内外游客,意在暗合97这个吉祥的数字,人们从这里不难看出作者借此表达爱国热情的良苦用心。相信作者的美意必将如愿以偿。通过这本摄影集,千千万万的人一定会把97这个光辉的页码和山青水秀、洞奇石美、桂花飘香的桂林风光永远留驻心间。

阳德华

1997年6月

POSTSCRIPT

　　When this selected photographic works comes out in the public, it is the time that the Hong Kong has returned to the Motherland and thus ending up the vicissitude and humiliation for one hundred years. To welcome that celebrating day by publishing this sellected photographic works is the primary intention of the author and the relevant editors. 97 is a fortunated figure which shall be no doubt a glorious page in Chinese national history, the Chinese all over the world shall be pround of that page and shall remember that page in generation and generation.

　　The author has selected 97 pieces from his more than ten thousands pieces of works to contribute to the broad masses of phtograph – loving people and tourists at home and abroad, implying the fortunating figure " 97 ", so people can feel easily the autor's patriotic enthusiasm by such expression and intention. I believe the author's intention and good willing shall be recognized and accepted by the public. Through this selected photographic works, hundred and thousand people shall remember 97 that glorious pages, on which integrated with the Guilin landscape where the hills are green, water is clear, cave is grotesque rock is wonderful and the air is heavy with the aroma of osmanthus, on their mind.

Yang Dehua

July, 1997

封面:青峰倒影

face cover: Inverted Reflection of Green Hil

表紙:青峰の倒影

封底:山在虚无飘渺

Back cover: Hills among visiona

里表紙:山は空虚でひょうびょうの

漓江导游图
Li River Scenic Spot

GUILIN
桂林

Tunnel Hill
穿山

Aged Banyan
老人古榕

Happy Marriage
at Biyan
碧岩喜结良缘

Elephant Trunk Hill
象鼻山

The Clean
净瓶山

Bottle Hill
瓶山

Forest of odd shaped Peaks
怪峰林立

Nine Oxen ridge
and three islets
九牛三洲

Strange
Husband Rock
夫妻石

Yearning for
望夫峰

Half-side Ferry
半边渡

Yang Di
杨堤

Beauty
of Crown Cave
冠岩奇景

Fresco Hill
画山

Wave Rock
浪石

The Lion Riding on A Car
骑车狮子

Xing Ping
兴坪

Yellow Cloth in The Water
黄布倒影

Snail Hill
螺蛳山

School Boy Hill
书童山

YANGSHUO
阳朔

Moon Hill
月亮山

Ancient Banyan Tree
古榕

The Green Lotus Peak
碧莲峰

Dragon Head Hill
龙头山